Kids
Communicate

Ann Rossi

PICTURE CREDITS
Cover (foreground, clockwise from right) © VCG/FPG, © David Young-Wolf/PhotoEdit, Norbert Schafer/The Stock Market, © Mary Kate Denny/PhotoEdit; (background, left to right) © Farrell Grehan/Photo Researchers, Inc., NY, Alan Klehr/Stone, page 1 Eliane Sulle/Image Bank; page 3 © David Lassman/The Image Works; pages 3 (left inset), 15 (top) © Arthur Tilley/FPG; page 3 (center inset) Mark Lewis/Stone; pages 3 (right inset), 28 Lloyd Wolf Photography, Arlington, VA; pages 4-5 Dennis Novak/Image Bank; page 5 Marc Grimberg/Image Bank; pages 6, 16 Superstock; pages 7, 9 (top), 14 (top) Granger Collection, NY; page 7 (inset) © Diane Padys/FPG; pages 8 (left-2), 9 (left-2), 25, 26 © Bettman/CORBIS; pages 8 (right-2), 9 (right) Corbis-Royalty-Free; p. 10 © Elizabeth Crews/The Image Works; page 11 © Farrell Grehan/Photo Researchers, Inc., NY; page 12 © National Geographic Society, Washington, DC; page 14 (inset) Andy Sacks/Stone; page 15 (right) © David Young-Wolf/PhotoEdit; page 15 (bottom) Archive Holdings/Image Bank; page 17 © Bob Daemmrich/The Image Works; page 18 J.P. Williams/Stone; page 19 Library of Congress; page 20 Ian Shaw/Stone; page 21 Michael S. Quinton/National Geographic Society, Image Collection; page 23 © Robert Maass/CORBIS; page 24 Courtesy Pensacola News Journal; page 27 Courtesy Hunter Scott; page 29 Joel Sartore/National Geographic Society, Image Collection; page 30 © Will Hart/PhotoEdit; back cover © Deborah Davis/PhotoEdit, Myrleen Cate/Stone, © VCG/FPG, Ken Chernus/FPG, Howard Kingsnorth/Stone

Produced through the worldwide resources of the National Geographic Society, John M. Fahey, Jr., President and Chief Executive Officer; Gilbert M. Grosvenor, Chairman of the Board; Nina D. Hoffman, Executive Vice President and President, Books and School Publishing.

PREPARED BY NATIONAL GEOGRAPHIC SCHOOL PUBLISHING
Ericka Markman, Vice President; Steve Mico, Editorial Director; Marianne Hiland, Editorial Manager; Anita Schwartz, Project Editor; Tara Peterson, Editorial Assistant; Jim Hiscott, Design Manager; Linda McKnight, Art Director; Diana Bourdrez, Anne Whittle, Photo Research; Matt Wascavage, Manager of Publishing Services; Sean Philpotts, Production Coordinator; Jane Ponton, Production Artist.

Production: Clifton M. Brown III, Manufacturing and Quality Control.

PROGRAM DEVELOPMENT
Gare Thompson Associates, Inc.

BOOK DESIGN
3r1 Group

Published by the National Geographic Society
1145 17th Street, N.W.
Washington, D.C. 20036-4688

ISBN-13: 978-0-7922-8689-9
ISBN-10: 0-7922-8689-8

Fifth Printing June, 2012
Printed in Canada.

Contents

How Do We Communicate?

Every day we get and share information. We talk to family and friends. We read newspapers, books, and magazines. We write letters and send e-mail messages. We watch television, listen to the radio, and use the Internet.

We communicate in many different ways at home, at school, and in the community. We communicate so often that we don't even think about it.

In how many different ways have you communicated today?

CHAPTER 1

Communication Firsts

We haven't always had so many ways to communicate. Many of the tools we use today were invented in the past 125 years. So, how did people communicate before then?

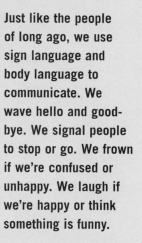

Just like the people of long ago, we use sign language and body language to communicate. We wave hello and good-bye. We signal people to stop or go. We frown if we're confused or unhappy. We laugh if we're happy or think something is funny.

We don't really know when humans began to speak. Experts who study languages think that early people first used sounds and body language to communicate with each other. They probably used sounds that imitated sounds in nature, such as the howling of the wind.

Later, people used fire, smoke signals, and drumbeats to send simple messages. They made drawings and painted pictures to tell a story. Eventually, people developed alphabets and writing systems. Then, they could write stories, send messages, and keep records.

Inventing Ways to Communicate

For centuries, books were handwritten and very expensive. There weren't many of them. In the mid-1400s, European printers began to use the movable-type printing press. For the first time, multiple copies of a book could be printed quickly. Books became more common and cheaper.

More people learned to read. Printing became an important means of communication.

After the printing press, other means of communication were invented. The time needed to send and receive information became shorter and shorter. The timeline below highlights inventions that have changed the way people communicate over the past 150 years.

Highlights in Communications

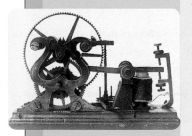

1840

The Electric Telegraph
The telegraph became more useful when Samuel Morse invented a code for the alphabet. Each letter was represented by a series of dots and dashes.

1876 **The Telephone**
Alexander Graham Bell was the first to patent a kind of telephone. Before the telephone, long-distance communication took a long time. You couldn't talk directly with someone. You could write letters or send a telegram, but you had to wait for a reply.

1895 **Movies**
The first movies were shown in Paris, France. By 1900, short movies called "newsreels" were shown before the main feature. People could now see moving pictures of events and places that they could only imagine before.

1907 **Radio**
Engineers developed a device which could pick up radio signals. By the early 1920s, there were radio stations throughout the United States. Millions of people listened in for news and entertainment.

A printer turns a huge screw on a printing press to push type against paper.

1946 **The Computer**
Two engineers built the first electronic digital computer. They called it ENIAC. In 1975, the first personal computer, the Altair, was designed.

1936 **Television**
The British Broadcasting Corporation (BBC) made the world's first TV broadcast. But television did not become a popular source of entertainment until the 1950s.

1969 **The Internet**
The United States Department of Defense developed an early version of the Internet in 1969. They called it ARPANET. It linked government defense computer networks. People could write e-mails (short for electronic mail) to others and receive vast amounts of information from around the world with great speed.

1980s **Fax machines**
Manufacturers developed facsimile (fax) machines that were smaller, cheaper, and faster than those invented earlier. Fax machines send and receive words and pictures over telephone lines.

Communicating in the Information Age

You live in the Information Age. Communicating should be easy. That's not always true! There are so many sources of information that it's easy to become confused. There are so many different ways to communicate that you need good communication skills.

Communication is about messages. Someone wants to let someone know something—the message. Most of our communication is personal communication. There are many ways we communicate with just one person or with people.

Personal Communication

- conversations
- letters
- e-mail
- notes
- telephone
- fax
- telegram

Sometimes we want to reach many people at the same time. So, we use **mass communication.** Here are some of the ways we can communicate a message to many people.

Mass Communication

- books, newspapers, magazines
- billboards and signs
- television
- radio
- movies and videos
- speeches, lectures
- computers and World Wide Web
- photographs, drawings, and paintings

People usually choose a way to communicate based on three factors: how fast it is, how much it costs, and how easy it is to use. Some ways to communicate are more useful at times than others. If you want to keep in touch with your brother who is away at school, you might call, e-mail, or write him a letter. If your class wants to let the community know what's happening in your school, you might publish a newsletter or create a Web page.

What are the different ways to communicate information?

Print Media

There are different kinds of **media,** or ways of communication. Print media are ways of communicating that are printed. Here are some common types of print media. Can you think of others?

- books
- magazines
- newspapers
- encyclopedias and almanacs
- brochures and flyers
- posters and billboards

We use print media to find all kinds of information. We might read the local newspaper to learn about plans for building a new mall. We might look up facts for a report in books, almanacs, and encyclopedias. We might find out about a concert from a poster, a sign, or a flyer.

Knowing what kinds of information are in different print media helps you find what you need. Think about the list of media above. What different kinds of information would you find in each?

Be Book Smart

Did you know that most books can be sorted into two categories?

■ **Fiction**
Books that are fiction tell a story. While some parts of a story may be about real events, the author has made up the story. Fiction books are usually not good sources for researching factual information.

■ **Nonfiction**
Books that are nonfiction provide information. They are based on facts. All reference books—encyclopedias, atlases, dictionaries, textbooks—are nonfiction. These are good sources of information.

Computers and the Web

Computers have changed the way we communicate. We use them to "talk" to people nearby and far away. We use them to find all sorts of information. We can find information about almost anything on the Web.

Just because the Web is easy and fast to use doesn't mean that it is always the best source of information. Here are some things to keep in mind as you "surf the Web."

- **Anybody can post anything on the Web.** You don't have to be an expert to put information on the Web. Anyone can make a Web page. That means that you can't always trust the information you find on the Web. It might be true. It might not be true.
- **Web addresses give clues about the author of the page.** If you look at the address of a Web page, you can figure out something about the author. Information about the writer can help you judge how useful the information on the site might be.

Web address

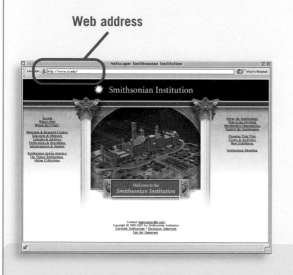

Look at the end of the Web address to figure out the source.

http//:www.si.edu

.com This often means that the source is a business. They may be trying to sell you a product or an idea that supports their business.

.org This means that the source is an organization. Many organizations are formed to support an idea or a cause. They are not formed to make money the way a business does.

.edu This means that the source is an educational group. It may be a college or a group formed to support education. You might find expert sources on these sites.

.gov This means that the source is the government. The government supplies a wide range of information that can be useful.

- The first true computers were based on military research begun during World War II. ENIAC, one of the first computers, weighed tons and stretched around the walls of a room that was 30 feet by 50 feet (9 meters by 15 meters) in size. Today's desktop, laptop, and notebook computers are smaller, more powerful, and faster than the huge ENIAC.
- The first actual computer bug was a moth. It flew into a computer and caused it to break down. People used tweezers to remove the moth. Today, people often refer to problems with computer programs as "bugs."

Web Safety Tips

The Web is a great tool for communicating, but you need to be smart about how you use it. You wouldn't invite strangers into your house. On the Web, don't invite strangers into your life. Use these tips to stay safe while on the Web.

- **DON'T give your last name, your address, or your phone number.** If you chat with people on the Web, keep the communication on the Web. Don't tell them how to reach you.
- **DON'T provide personal information about yourself or your family.** Personal information is just that—personal. If you feel uncomfortable about something that someone asks, don't answer. Tell a parent or another adult.
- **DON'T arrange to meet strangers.** Just because you've talked to someone on the Web doesn't mean you know him or her. Remember, people can communicate anything on the Web. You can't tell what's true and what's not.
- **DO keep an adult informed.** You tell your parents where you are going and with whom you are going. Do the same when on the Web. Let them know which chat rooms you spend time in.

Telephones

Think about what life would be like without the telephone. You couldn't call your friends. You couldn't call to get directions to a party. You couldn't even call to order a pizza!

Even though you probably use the phone many times a day, there are still some things to keep in mind. When you use the phone, listen carefully and speak clearly. You want to be sure that you hear everything that is said. You want to be sure the person you are calling hears everything you have to say.

Listening Tips
- Listen carefully to what the speaker is saying.
- Take notes if you are getting information.
- Do not interrupt the speaker.
- Ask the speaker to repeat something if it is unclear.

Speaking Tips
- Speak clearly so that you can be heard.
- Do not mumble or scream.
- Be polite.
- If a stranger calls, don't give out personal information. Don't tell your name or address. Don't tell who is at home. Offer to take a message and then have an adult return the call.

Movies and Television

When was the last time you turned on the TV or popped a movie into the VCR or DVD? Did you watch an animated cartoon, a comedy, or an adventure? We watch television, videos, and movies for entertainment. We also watch these media to learn about the world around us.

Television lets us see history in the making. We can watch sports, political debates, trials, and even wars as they take place. We watch events in our own communities as well as in other countries around the world. We also learn about events, both past and present, by watching a special type of movie, called a **documentary.**

Radio

Radio was the first mass broadcast media. Radio reached millions of people and changed communications forever. Today, we can listen to news programs, music, talk shows, speeches, and live interviews from around the world.

When you listen for information, listen carefully. Remember, you can't ask announcers to repeat what they've said! You can send away for a **transcript,** or written document, that tells what was said on the program. You can also tape-record a radio show.

✓Tips

for Viewing

When watching television or movies to get information, remember these tips.
- Listen carefully.
- Take notes to remember key points.
- Pay attention to important details.
- Note how the pictures support what you hear.

for Listening

Keep in mind that some radio talk shows give listeners a chance to express their opinions on different issues. The callers are telling what they think or believe about something. These opinions are not facts. They cannot be proven to be true or correct.

CHAPTER 3

Evaluating Information

Finding information in today's world is easy. There are many sources to turn to. The challenge is figuring out what information you can trust. How can you tell if information you hear or read is useful or useless?

Should you believe everything you read, hear, or see?

How to Evaluate Information

The information that you read, hear, and see can change you. It can change what you know about something. It can change the way you feel about something. It can even make you take action.

That's why it is important for you to **evaluate**, or judge, the information you find. You need to make sure the information you receive is **reliable.** You can trust reliable information. You can count on it to be true.

Use Reliable Sources

How do you decide if a source is reliable?

Reliable information is accurate. It comes from people who know more than most people about a topic. These people are called **experts.**

People might be experts for different reasons.

- Experts have witnessed or lived through an event or time that is important. If your grandfather was in the Vietnam War, he can tell you about his experiences there.
- Experts have studied a topic for a long time. A scientist who studies sharks would be an expert in shark behavior.
- Experts have a job that gives them a special view about a topic. A sports reporter may be an expert on the history of baseball.

Would these soldiers have been reliable sources for information about Civil War battles?

Ask these questions about the source of information to figure out if it is reliable.

- Is the author of this information an expert in the subject? What is the author's background?
- Is the author telling about his or her own experiences?
- Did the author actually witness the events described or know the people he or she describes?

Primary sources are original records and documents. They include letters, diaries, speeches, films, audio recordings, and photographs. Primary sources provide useful firsthand information. They give you a feeling for what life was like during a certain period in history.

Check It Out

You are doing a report on life in space. Which sources would you use?

- 👍 An interview in a science magazine with an astronaut who spent five months on the Russian space station
- 👍 The government website for NASA (National Aeronautics and Space Administration)
- 👎 An interview with the director of a science fiction movie

Use Up-to-Date Information

How can you tell if information is up-to-date?

Sometimes you need current, or up-to-date, information. This means you need the latest news and facts about a topic.

Check It Out

Your family is buying a new television. You want the most current information about the new models. Which sources would you use?

- 👍 The catalog from a store that sells televisions
- 👎 A consumer buying guide published two years ago
- 👍 A magazine article published two months ago that compares different brands of televisions

How can you tell whether a source is up-to-date?

- The copyright date for a book, magazine article, CD, or other media tells you when it was published or created. Check copyright dates. Recent dates mean that it is more likely to be up-to-date. You can find the copyright in the first few pages of a book. Check newspaper and magazine covers for their publication dates. Movie credits often list the year the film was produced.

- If a source includes a **bibliography,** or listing of the magazines and books used by an author, look at it. Check if the author has used sources with recent publication dates. If so, chances are better that the information is current.

- Sometimes websites don't tell you when information was posted or updated. Information left on a site for a long time can be out-of-date. If you don't know how old the information is, use another source to check your facts.

Identify Facts and Opinions

How can you tell if facts or opinions are being communicated?

Facts can be proven right or wrong. You can check facts in encyclopedias, almanacs, and in other sources. Facts include numbers, years, and names.

Opinions tell what a person thinks or believes. Sometimes opinions include words such as *think*, *feel*, *believe*, *should*, *may*, and *seem*. Opinions can be supported by facts, but they are still opinions.

Both facts and opinions can be useful. But, you need to know which statements are facts and which statements are opinions.

Tips

for Fact Checking

- Check facts before you use them. Use reliable sources such as encyclopedias, atlases, and almanacs. Make sure that the source is up-to-date.

- Use two sources to check your facts. Some sources make mistakes. So it's good to have a backup source.

Check It Out

You are writing an article for your class newspaper. You need to be clear about which statements are facts and which are opinions in your article. Look at the paragraph below. The writer was careful to show this.

Fact —— The gray wolf was reintroduced to Yellowstone National Park in 1995-1996.

Opinion { I believe that the gray wolf needs protection so that it will not become extinct. Others feel that the gray wolf will kill cattle and other livestock on nearby ranches.

Identify Point of View

Everybody has a point of view. You develop a point of view based on your experiences and what you already know.

To figure out another person's point of view, here are some things to consider.
- Why is this person or group telling me this information?
- What is its purpose?
- Does someone want to persuade me to do, think, or buy something?

It helps to figure out an author's or a speaker's point of view. An author may be telling you only those facts that support what he or she believes. The author might leave out other important facts. The information could be **biased,** or one-sided.

Here are some clues that information may be biased.
- Only one point of view is presented.
- No facts are included to support opinions.
- Some key facts are not included.
- Many questions are left unanswered.

Check It Out

You are doing a project on air pollution in your city. You find two websites with information you think you can use. Which source might be biased?

- **The chemical company nearby tells all the steps it is taking to cut down on air pollution. The company provides facts about how the air has improved since it started these steps.**
- **A government report gives another set of facts about the air quality. These facts tell that the air has improved a little, but it is still unhealthy for those living near the chemical plant.**

CHAPTER 4

Kids Take Action

People depend on information they can trust. They need trustworthy information to make good decisions and to understand the world around them. Many people, including young people, use information to make a difference in their communities and in the world.

Hunter Scott was 12 years old when he used his communication skills to correct a wrong. He began by researching and evaluating information. Then, he communicated the information he found to powerful people.

It all started when Hunter saw the movie *Jaws*. A character in the movie told about the sinking of the U.S.S. *Indianapolis*. He told how the survivors spent four days and five nights in shark infested waters before they were rescued. Hunter decided to use the sinking of the *Indianapolis* as the topic for a history report. Here's the information he found.

The Disaster

It was the summer of 1945. The *Indianapolis*, with 1,200 men on board, was on a secret mission during World War II. It had sailed from San Francisco to an island in the South Pacific. After dropping off key parts for the atomic bomb that would end the war with Japan, the ship set out for the Philippine Islands. A Japanese submarine torpedoed the ship, which sank in 12 minutes. This attack turned out to be one of the worst wartime disasters in the history of the U.S. Navy.

About 300 men went down with the ship. Another 900 waited in the Pacific waters for rescue teams. No one came for five nights and four days. By then, only 316 men were left alive. The others had died from lack of drinking water, exposure to the weather, or shark attacks.

Hunter Scott poses with the jaws of a shark.

U.S.S. *Indianapolis*

The Blame

The captain of the ship, Charles
Butler McVay III, survived the
disaster and was blamed for it. He
was found guilty of putting his ship
in danger while the nation was at war.

The Controversy

Many of the survivors felt that
their captain was not guilty. But
what could they do? Over time,
new information about the disaster
was released. More and more people
started to think the captain was not
guilty.

Captain Charles McVay III

Getting the Facts

While researching the sinking of the *Indianapolis,* Hunter read about the captain's **court-martial.** He found one book that claimed the captain was unfairly blamed. Hunter decided to focus his research on the captain.

Hunter came across a list of survivors. He knew that these people were reliable sources. They had witnessed what had happened at sea. He contacted many of them and learned that most shared the opinion that the captain had been treated unfairly.

Hunter continued to dig for facts. He learned that at least three Navy locations had received SOS signals from the *Indianapolis.* These signals were either ignored or thought to be a Japanese trick.

New Evidence

New evidence became public. It showed that the U.S. Navy had cracked the secret code of the Japanese messages. It knew that a Japanese submarine was along the path of the *Indianapolis,* but never told the captain that a submarine was near his ship. The Navy did not want the Japanese to find out that the Navy had cracked their code. The Navy's point of view, at the time, was to keep this information secret.

Survivors of the *Indianapolis* leave a Navy hospital ship to go ashore.

Maurice Bell, one of the survivors, shows Hunter Scott his Purple Heart.

The Final Chapter

Senator Bob Smith from New Hampshire carefully read Hunter Scott's research. The Senator then met with Hunter and some survivors to discuss the disaster. Based on Hunter's research and the survivors' **testimony,** Senator Smith became convinced that Captain McVay had been wrongly blamed. He felt that a wrong should be corrected.

As a result, the U.S. Senate held hearings to review the case against Captain McVay. The House of Representatives had already declared the "guilty" verdict of Captain McVay to be completely unjust.

Hunter Scott at a press conference in Washington, D.C.

The Senate stated the captain was not to blame. Hunter Scott, with his curiosity and research skills, helped clear the name of an innocent man.

You may not be able to change history, but you too can make a difference. You can use what you've learned about evaluating information to become better informed.

Once you have determined what information is credible and accurate, you can share this information with others. You can communicate information that you know is reliable and trustworthy. Here are some steps you can follow.

Step 1: Choose Your Message

Every form of communication has a message. What do you want to say to others? How will you present your message to others? Think about an issue that matters to you.

Model

Mr. Stanley's fourth-grade class was studying endangered species. They read in the news that the gray wolf might be taken off the endangered species list. They became very interested and decided to research the facts behind this story.

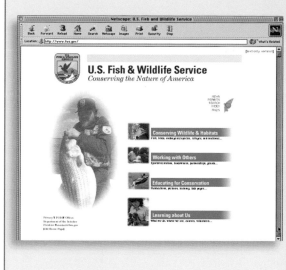

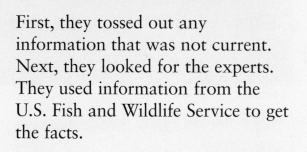

Step 2: Collect and Evaluate Information

Check out a wide range of sources —books, magazines, videos, the World Wide Web, and any experts you can interview. Be smart about your sources.

- Find the experts.
- Use up-to-date sources.
- Sort out facts from opinions.
- Be aware of different points of view.

Model
The class found lots of information about the gray wolf. It seemed like many people and groups were interested in this issue. They decided to use some guidelines to sort through this mountain of information.

First, they tossed out any information that was not current. Next, they looked for the experts. They used information from the U.S. Fish and Wildlife Service to get the facts.

Then, they sorted out the facts from the opinions. There were many opinions! Finally, they thought about the different points of view. They found groups that objected to wolves because they killed cattle and other livestock. They also found other groups that supported the wolves being reintroduced through national parks and other areas.

Step 3: Decide how to Communicate Information

Now that you have your information, it's time to decide how you want to communicate it to others. Will you write an article for the school newspaper? Will you create a page on the Web or a multimedia presentation? Choose a way that will help you present what you've learned in a clear, interesting way.

Model

With Mr. Stanley's help, the class created a Web page. On this page they included the facts they found as well as pictures, maps showing the wolf's natural habitat, and graphs showing wolf populations over time. The class agreed that they'd like to update the page during the school year. They intend to stay current on this topic!

Glossary

biased holding a strong feeling for or against a person or issue without enough reason

bibliography a list of books and magazines on a subject

court-martial a military trial

documentary a movie or television program made about real situations and people

e-mail electronic mail

evaluate to judge

expert a person who knows more than most people about a topic

fact a piece of information that is true or real and can be proven right or wrong

fiction stories about characters and events that are not real

mass communication the process of reaching many people at the same time

media ways of communicating, such as newspapers or television

nonfiction information about real things, people, and events

opinion a belief that is based on what a person thinks rather than what is proven or known to be true

point of view a way of looking at things

primary source original documents and records, such as letters, diaries, and speeches

reliable accurate or trustworthy

testimony a statement made under oath

transcript a printed copy of what was said on a radio or television broadcast or in court

Index